D1434216

THIS JOURNAL BELONGS TO

....

Copyright © 2022 by Hay House, Inc.

Published in the United States by:
Hay House, Inc.: www.hayhouse.com®

Published in Australia by:
Hay House Australia Pty. Ltd.: www.hayhouse.com.au

Published in the United Kingdom by:
Hay House UK, Ltd.: www.hayhouse.co.uk

Published in India by:
Hay House Publishers India: www.hayhouse.co.in

Cover & interior design: Ashley Prine, Tandem Books
Cover Illustration: © Claire Bremner
Image Credits: Shutterstock: Back cover & interior decorative elements used throughout © Romanova Ekaterina; 13, 77, 91, 105 © Lovely Mandala; 35 © Tancha; 36 © Katika; 51 (top and bottom) © Tatiana Goncharuk; 51 (center) © Igor Vyunyshev; 67 (figure) © kichikimi; 67 (hand) © Viktoriia_M; 71 © sliplee; 76 © Aleksandr Gladkiy; 104 © EasterBunny; 112 (rosemary) © Hudozhnica_Ananas; 112 (mint, cinnamon, lemon) © katieromanoff_art; 113 © IrinaKrivoruchko; 98, 99 © Tata.Ya.

Tradepaper ISBN: 978-1-4019-6756-7

10 9 8 7 6 5 4 3 2 1

1st edition, July 2022

Printed in the United States of America

MORNING MEDITATIONS

Journal

POSITIVE PROMPTS & AFFIRMATIONS
TO START YOUR DAY

The Hay House Editors

HAY HOUSE, INC.
Carlsbad, California • New York City
London • Sydney • New Delhi

INTRODUCTION

GOOD MORNING, YOU!

And welcome to your new daily practice of meditation and journaling!

This journal is designed to be your personal companion for deepening your meditation experience. Whether you're new to meditation, familiar with it and looking to build a more regular practice, or already meditating regularly and want to explore and expand your repertoire, this journal will guide you to a morning routine that is tailored to your own preferences and interests.

Meditation has gained more and more acceptance over the years as a beneficial practice for the body, mind, and soul. It has been shown to help manage stress, increase your powers of concentration and memory, make you more creative, crystalize your sense of purpose, and improve your overall well-being. Mornings are an especially powerful time to meditate, because you can get your day off to a positive, intentional start. Taking time to breathe, reflect, and care for yourself can help you face the day's challenges, energize you for what's to come, and allow you to bring into focus what's important to you each and every day.

While everyone can benefit from meditation, there's not a one-size-fits-all practice. There are lots of different ways to meditate, from the classic practice of sitting in silence to turning everyday

chores into meditative moments. It's good to explore what's out there to find what suits you best. Writing about your meditation experiences helps you become mindful of what you like, what works for you, and how you're benefiting from your practice. It also helps keep you motivated and coming back to sit every day.

In this guided journal, you'll find exercises to help you build your morning meditation practice by creating the time and space you need to realistically fit it into your schedule and household. You'll explore meditations that help you awaken your insight, heal old wounds, prepare for a big day, generate energy, build gratitude, live mindfully, repeat mantras and affirmations, and so much more. Guided prompts will introduce you to practices such as Transcendental Meditation, Zazen, movement and object meditation, visualization, and tapping. You'll also find interesting info on meditation companions like crystals, essential oils, herbs, and chakras so you can see if you like bringing them into your practice.

Journaling about these different ways of meditating as you try them will deepen the experience and help you build a lasting practice that you'll look forward to every sunrise. With plenty of space to write and even doodle and color, these meditations will help you greet each morning, so you can live each day mindfully, gratefully, and intentionally. Namaste!

A *GOOD* MORNING MEDITATION

A morning meditation is like having a good breakfast: it gives you the energy you need to do all that you have to do in your day. And just like a good breakfast, the best meditation practice may be different from person to person. Some people feel their best after something quick and light, while others like to take their time with a nourishing sit-down.

With that in mind, think about what you want from your morning meditation practice. What would you like it to look like, and what do you hope it does for your day? Try to free yourself from any preconceived ideas of what it should be and write about what a good morning meditation could mean for you.

....

....

....

....

....

....

....

MORNING ROUTINE

*M*orning meditations are great because they bring clarity, focus, and a bit of peace to your day. To build a morning meditation practice that sticks, it's best if you can work it into your existing routine. That means carving out time in what can be a busy part of the day.

What's your morning routine like? Make a list of your general schedule.

....

....

....

....

....

....

....

....

Where in that routine can you work in time for meditation? Maybe you can find the time while the coffee is brewing, or if you hit snooze, you can meditate in bed during those nine minutes in blanket heaven. What appeals to you?

"MY FIRST THOUGHTS
ON AWAKENING
BEFORE I OPEN
MY EYES ARE TO
BE THANKFUL FOR
EVERYTHING I CAN
THINK OF."

–Louise Hay

FIRST THOUGHTS

What are the very first thoughts that come into your head when you wake? Write them out as quickly as you can in total free-form. Don't try to make sense of them; just write.

....

....

....

....

....

....

....

....

....

....

....

continued . . .

Read what you wrote. Are your thoughts full of gratitude and love, or are they more focused on the needs of the day and the stress those bring? Do they feel clear and intentional this morning or disordered and muddled? What would you like your first thoughts to be about? Write about that. Then as you go to sleep tonight, spend some time meditating on the thoughts you'd like to have when you wake. In the morning, take note of how quickly those thoughts surface.

ZEN OUT

THIS IS YOUR SPOT

*C*arving out time for yourself to meditate in the morning is in itself an expression of self-love and care, and having a safe space to meditate is an important part of that. This space doesn't need to be a spotless white room with a single cushion in the center. It just needs to be a place where you feel comfortable and secure and can meditate undisturbed.

What feeling would you like to have wash over you each time you enter your meditation space?

....

....

....

....

....

....

....

....

Sketch a picture of your ideal morning meditation spot. It can be a real space or somewhere fantastical. Let your morning mind run with it!

MAKING TIME FOR MORNING MEDITATIONS

There are a few easy things you can do at night to help you carve out time to meditate in the morning without feeling like you're just squeezing it into an already-busy schedule. Not only will these practices help you make the time, but you'll go to sleep with the good intention of your next meditation in your heart.

Set the scene: Give the place where you meditate a once-over. Clean it of clutter, fluff up your cushions, and maybe even give it a little spritz of essential oil to make it a welcoming space that you can enter in the morning with no muss or fuss.

Plan ahead: Pick out what meditation you'd like to do in the morning. That might mean selecting one from this journal, choosing one online or on an app, knowing the affirmation on which you'd like to meditate, or using any other method of selection that you enjoy.

Gather what you need: Bring whatever you'll need for the meditation to the spot where you plan to sit. If the meditation involves a writing exercise, or you like to journal before or after you sit, place your journal and pen or pencil there. If it's a crystal or other type of object meditation, set that out the night before.

Set up to save time: Is there any part of your morning ritual that you can prepare for at night so that you have more time in the morning? Maybe you can set the timer on your coffee maker to percolate while you meditate. Or if you're more of a morning smoothie person, you could put your ingredients in the blender and store that in the fridge overnight, so all you have to do in the morning is turn it on.

Let the house know: Explain to those you live with that your morning meditation practice is important to you and ask that they give you this time to yourself as an expression of their love and appreciation for you.

Make a list of the things you can prepare in advance to make sure you have time to meditate in the morning.

....

....

....

....

....

....

....

....

....

....

GOOD INTENTIONS

*O*ne of the great things about meditating in the morning is that it gives you an opportunity to set an intention for the day. Whether it's a specific goal you want to meet or a general mindset you'd like to have, such as gratitude or taking things a little less seriously, reflecting on it first thing can help bring focus to your day.

Take a few minutes to write down your reflections on what you want your intention to be for the day. Then distill it into a single, clear phrase—like an affirmation or mantra—and meditate on it.

Now write it out 10 more times.

"LISTEN TO YOUR
HEART AND TRUST
THE DIRECTION YOU
ARE BEING PULLED.
SOMETHING INSIDE
YOU ALREADY KNOWS
WHAT TO DO."

–Spring Washam

AWAKENING YOUR POWER

This morning, focus on the awakening power of this quote from Spring Washam's *Fierce Heart*. Meditate on it for 5 or 10 minutes or longer—however long you like to use in your current practice. Try to listen to your heart with a real openness to possibility. See if you can hear that wise voice that knows the way, that intuition that sometimes is so quiet you aren't sure if you heard it right. What did you hear? The more you listen for it and trust it, the clearer it will become.

OBJECT MEDITATION

Often when we meditate, we center our attention on the breath, sounds, or other sensations in the body to keep the mind focused and present, but there are so many things we can choose as a focal point. Find a small, beloved object. One that brings you joy. Get into a comfortable position, close your eyes, and meditate on this object with your hands. Feel its details, its texture, its increasing warmth from your hands. Make it the focus of your attention, reflecting on either the feel of the object or its meaning to you, whichever holds your attention best.

Draw your chosen object below and surround it with the words you associate with it.

COCK-A-DOODLE-DO

Let your creativity flow freely this morning! Doodle to your heart's content on this page, filling it with any patterns, shapes, or images you feel drawn to this morning.

AFFIRMATIONS FOR ABUNDANCE

"I am aligned with the energy of abundance."

"I am worthy of what I desire."

"I accept and receive abundance."

We all deserve abundance in love, in prosperity, in money, in health, in safety, in happiness, and in all that we desire. To obtain abundance in any and all areas of your life, you have to believe this is true, not just for others, not just in general, but for you. Meditating on an abundance affirmation in the morning is especially powerful, but only if the affirmation rings true for you. That is why it is important to choose them carefully, change them to suit your own voice, or even write your own.

What abundance are you looking to attract? Write about it with some detail. Freely explore what abundance means to you. Then distill from that longer journal entry a brief affirmation that resonates with you down to your core.

....

....

....

....

....

....

"TO STUDY THE BUDDHA WAY IS TO STUDY THE SELF, TO STUDY THE SELF IS TO FORGET THE SELF, AND TO FORGET THE SELF IS TO BE ENLIGHTENED BY THE TEN THOUSAND THINGS."

–Zen Master Dōgen

ZAZEN IN THE MORNING

Zazen meditation follows the Buddhist tradition of seeking enlightenment through the recognition that all things are one. This morning, try to embrace that universal unity. Sit in a comfortable but alert position. Bring your gaze to rest gently on the floor in front of you. Allow your breath to come naturally through the nose. Focus your attention on the breath in and count each one on the inhale up to 10 and then down again, repeating this for as long as you like. If your attention wanders, bring it back to the breath gently and without judgment. Let thoughts and distractions pass by, like clouds before the sun. Recognize the body, the breath, the mind; they are all one thing.

How do you feel after this meditation? One tiny step closer to enlightenment?

MORNING LIGHT

Getting some sunlight in the morning has been proven to be beneficial in a number of ways: it can help with issues like insomnia, PMS, and even seasonal affective disorder. This meditation will help you get some of those good golden rays.

Find a spot near a window that lets in some of that glorious, new morning light, or choose a comfortable place to sit outside. Position yourself so you're facing east as best you can. Set a timer for 5 or 10 minutes and play some meditation music if you wish. Close your eyes and lift your face toward the morning light. Feel its warmth on your skin. Breathe the energy of the morning sunlight into your nose, your throat, lungs, and body. Feel it suffuse into your system. Once you are settled in your breathing, focus your attention on the light coming in through your closed eyelids. Watch the patterns that emerge there. If your thoughts drift somewhere, gently bring them back to the warm, energizing light.

How did this meditation feel in your body? How are your mood and your energy?

....

....

....

....

....

BODY CHECK-IN

$\mathcal{S}$ay good morning to your self with a body scan. Start by getting into your favorite meditation position and closing your eyes. Take a few steady, intentional breaths. Then send your awareness to the top of your head. Now slowly send that awareness down, checking in with your scalp, your ears, your eyes, and so on, sending it through each part of your body. You might feel a little tingling in your hands, a sore muscle, or the pressure of your body connecting to the floor, chair, or bed.

What did you notice on your scan? Do any parts feel particularly good? Do any parts need a little love and care? Draw your body on the next page and use colors or write notes to indicate how different parts of your body feel.

....

....

....

....

....

....

....

BURN OFF THE FOG

Sometimes you need a little help burning off the brain fog in the morning, and this visualization exercise is just the thing. Get into your favorite meditation position and take a few energizing breaths. Picture a thick, gray fog all around you. Straight ahead you see a light coming up over the horizon. Vibrant shades of pink and yellow begin to burn the fog away. As the gorgeous golden sphere of the sun rises, the fog disappears, revealing a lush, beautiful landscape.

Draw your landscape here. Fill the space with color and texture. Don't worry about getting it to look perfect; just make sure it feels right while you do it.

"IF YOU TAKE HEALING
INTERVALS, YOU'RE
GIVING YOURSELF A LIVE
MESSAGE. IT WILL HELP
YOU. THE FACT THAT YOU
FEEL WORTHWHILE, THAT
YOU DESERVE THE TIME, IS
A MESSAGE UNTO ITSELF."

–Bernie S. Siegel, M.D.

A HEALING INTERVAL

According to Dr. Siegel, meditations are "healing intervals" that help you process and heal your past as well as prepare you to deal with the stress and challenges of the coming day. This morning, sit or lie in your favorite meditation position. Put on some calming music, close your eyes, and breathe in life. Check in with your body and breathe energy and healing into any places that are sore or strained. Breathe cleansing breaths to clear your mind of any lingering thoughts or problems so you can start your day fresh. Allow a healing wave of colors to wash over you and cleanse you of any stress or pain.

Color in your healing, cleansing wave below in the hues you envisioned. What do those colors feel like to you?

A MORNING MANTRA

Mantras are tools that concentrate your thoughts, like a magnifying glass focusing the diffused light of the sun into a powerful beam. They are ancient in origin, dating back thousands of years to the Vedic scriptures in India and they have appeared through time as anything from a single powerful symbol—om—to short prayers and affirmations.

Repeating a mantra aloud and with rhythm is a special kind of meditation that can send a buzzing through the body and soul, awakening you to energy, purpose, creativity, or whatever you are chanting for. Here are a few popular mantras and their translations when helpful. (You may recognize the last three from the works of Louise Hay.)

Om: A sacred sound whose vibration signifies ultimate consciousness and reality.

Aham Prema: Pronounced *ah-hahm pray-ma*, this translates to "I am divine love."

Om Shanti, Shanti, Shanti: "Om peace, peace, peace."

Lokah Samastah Sukhino Bhavantu: Pronounced *lo-kah sah-mah-stah soo-kee-no bah-vahn-too*, this translates to "May all beings everywhere be happy and free."

Lumen de Lumine: Pronounced *loo-min duh loo-meen*, this translates to "The light from light."

May I be happy. May I be well.

I am that I am.

All is well in my world.

Life loves me.

I am healthy, whole, and complete.

Try writing some of your own mantras. They can be favorite prayers or affirmations or even a sound or sequence of sounds that just feels good to say aloud.

....

....

....

....

....

....

....

....

....

....

....

BREATHE IN ENERGY

$\mathcal{S}$ettle into your favorite meditation position and begin to focus on your breathing. As you inhale, feel all that energizing oxygen filling your lungs, entering your bloodstream, and coursing through your body. As you exhale, breathe out any sensations of tiredness or heaviness you brought with you out of sleep. With each breath, feel your energy level rise another notch.

How do you feel? What's your energy level like on a scale of 1 to 10?

1   2   3   4   5   6   7   8   9   10

....

....

....

....

....

....

....

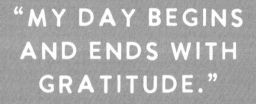

"MY DAY BEGINS
AND ENDS WITH
GRATITUDE."

–Louise Hay

GRATITUDE EVERYWHERE

*S*tart the morning by meditating on what you are grateful for. Think about all the things, big and small, that fill your heart with joy and gratitude and write them here.

Once you have a good list going, consider writing a gratitude affirmation, like "I'm so grateful for _____ !" on some sticky notes and posting them around your home in places like inside the fridge, your sock drawer, and the medicine cabinet. The exercise of sticking these notes directly on all the things you are grateful for will bring a keen mindfulness of the gratitude you have for the many blessings in your life that you might sometimes overlook.

MOVEMENT MEDITATION

*B*ringing movement into your morning meditation can be an energizing way to start the day. Stand up tall with your feet a little more than hip-width apart. Inhale as you draw your hands up toward your chest and hold them together in prayer hands. Exhale as you bring your hands down and gently bend your knees. Repeat this movement with your breath a few times and then start to sway with it, moving side to side as you rise with the inhale and root down with your exhales. Connect your breath to the movement and allow it to flow. There is no right way to do this, only what's right for you.

How do you feel? Scan your body to see if you notice any sensations, like a tingling in the hands or a liveliness in your muscles. Do you feel differently than before you did this movement meditation?

....

....

....

....

....

....

MAKE YOUR OWN RITUALS

We go through so many of the same motions every day: making the bed, brewing tea, washing dishes, drinking water, sweeping the floor. We often think of these things as chores, but with a small shift in thinking, you can make them into meditative rituals.

List some things that you do so often you do them by rote. Write down a couple of details about the actual motions and sensations of performing these acts. The sound of water running, the rhythm of the broom swishing, the satisfaction of finishing the dishes. Then, the next time you perform one of these daily "chores," treat it as a meditative ritual by focusing on the act of care and being. You may decide not to turn all of these acts into rituals, but you will find at least a couple more opportunities for meditative moments in your routine.

....

....

....

....

....

....

"IF YOU WANT TO REACH OUT FOR SOMETHING GREATER, YOU HAVE TO LET GO OF WHAT'S IN YOUR HAND."

–Sonia Choquette

LET IT GO

What have you been holding on to even though it doesn't serve you? A relationship, anger at someone, an idea about success, a goal that comes from without instead of within? This morning, you can meditate on letting it go.

Write down the negative things you're holding on to. Then, take some deep cleansing breaths and start to cross out all those things as you begin to let them go. Finally scrawl affirmations or draw flowers and hearts over the list, and add whatever your soul desires to wipe out what you want to let go of so you can be open to receiving something greater.

IT'S CALLED MEDITATION PRACTICE FOR A REASON

When meditating, you've probably experienced distracting sounds, feelings, thoughts. They steal your attention away, making you feel frustrated and annoyed, like you're "not doing it right." Here's a secret: This happens to pretty much everyone. Allowing your thoughts and the world to be what they are, warts and all, is one of the deeply gratifying benefits of meditation. Instead of punishing yourself and fighting against these lingering thoughts or trying to control them in some way, practice letting them pass without judgment. And as you get better at practicing this calm composure while you meditate, you may find this attitude comes to you even when you're not meditating.

This morning, take a give yourself minutes to just sit and take the meditation as it comes, no judgments. Perhaps you rest your attention on the breath or a sound—or not. Let distractions come and go as they please. This is just practice.

How did this meditation feel? When a distraction came up, how did you react to it?

....

....

....

....

ENERGIZING CRYSTALS

Crystals each have their own energy, their own vibration. Some are good listeners, absorbing the energy you put into them (I'm looking at you, clear quartz), while others are packed with healing and energy. By adding crystals to your morning meditation practice, you can charge your day with an energy boost, courtesy of Mother Nature. Here are some crystals you can try:

Quartz of any color is good for an energy boost and for upping your vitality. It also amplifies the energy of other crystals.

Poppy Jasper is energizing and clarifying, driving away grogginess like a shot of espresso.

Aventurine is both stress-reducing and energizing—win-win!

Citrine will fill your creative energy tank while releasing negativity.

Amber boosts your positivity and gives you the energy to get things done.

Ruby is thought to recharge your energy by increasing blood flow.

While different crystals do have specific energies, it's always a good idea to let your intuition guide you to your crystals. If you open yourself up to that intuition, it can feel as if the crystals choose you! When you first bring a new crystal into your practice, you should cleanse it of any energy it's picked up from people along its way to you. You can do this in one of three ways: by passing it through smoke, letting it sit on a windowsill to absorb sun and moonlight for 24 hours, or pouring fresh water over it.

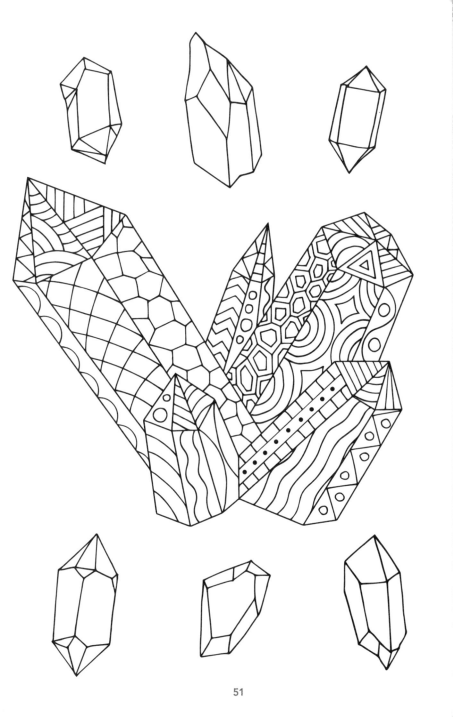

A CRYSTAL CLEAR MORNING

You can bring crystals into your morning meditation in a few ways. You can lie down and place crystals on any or all of your chakra points (see page 98), you can sit and hold crystals in your hand, or you can arrange them around you. Whatever way you choose to do it, meditate on the energy of each crystal, imagining its energy absorbing into you and coursing through your body, driving negativity out. Light in, dark out.

How did you choose to do this meditation? Draw the orientation of your crystals below and then write about how you felt during and after the meditation.

"I AM NOT JUST MY BODY,
I AM NOT JUST THIS
EARTH. I SURRENDER TO
THE VASTNESS OF SPIRIT,
TO THE INFINITY OF LOVE,
TO THE ECSTASY OF THE
UNEXPECTED, AND TO THE
BOUNTY OF HAPPINESS
I DESERVE."

– Judith Orloff, M.D.

SURRENDER

We often think of surrender as a giving in to greater forces than ourselves, but in fact the hardest thing to surrender is the masks we wear, the control we try to have. We show a version of ourselves we think people want to see instead being our authentic selves. We wake up each day thinking about all the things we should do or we have to do, without reflecting on what our real purpose is in life and if those actions will serve it. Take time this morning to meditate on listening to the calling life has for you. Try to hear what your real purpose is and think about what actions you can take today to serve that calling.

What did this meditation reveal? In what ways can you surrender that will allow you to show up as your most authentic self?

....

....

....

....

....

....

....

RELAXED AND READY

This is it. The big day! You've got a presentation to give, you're starting something new, or you're ending something old. You're buzzing with anticipation, and perhaps that excitement (or dread, no judgments) is tipping over into anxiety. This exercise will help you relax and ready yourself.

Write down any fears you have about today in the left column. Let your mind catastrophize the heck out of it, so you can see that no matter what happens, it's not the literal end of the world. Then close your eyes, take some deep breaths, and envision the opposite. In your mind, picture everything going the best it possibly can. Now let your mind run in this direction, and this time, visualize and make it feel as real as you can. In the right column, write the positive, best-case outcome that's at the other end of each of your fears.

Worst Case	Best Case
....	....
....	....
....	....
....	....
....	....
....	....

Worst Case

....

....

....

....

....

....

....

....

....

....

....

....

Best Case

....

....

....

....

....

....

....

....

....

....

....

....

FREE YOURSELF

Many meditations focus the mind on something, whether it be the breath, a mantra, or even the clearing of the mind to be as thought-free as possible. The goal of this meditation is just the opposite. Instead of trying to hone a sense of control or focus, you have permission to set aside all that effort for a bit and just be. Settle into your favorite meditation with your eyes opened or closed and just be. Let your thoughts run free without judging them. Don't try to focus or control them. Sit for as long as you like and allow yourself to be free.

Where else in your day can you bring in a little more freedom? What are you trying to control that, for one reason or another, just isn't worth that effort?

....

....

....

....

....

....

....

AWAKEN YOUR INNER SIGHT

The deep stillness of meditation can help you find answers to questions through insight—a deep inner awareness that knows so much. We just need to wake up this sense that can easily be obscured by the ever-chattering monkey brain. This morning, write down a question that is weighing on you, whether it be about relationships, your path, love, spirituality, or any other area. Then, sit in meditation for as long as you like. No need to ponder the question. Instead, focus your attention on the spot just above and between your brows, where the third eye is said to reside.

When you come out of your meditation, write free-form, in a stream of consciousness way, about your question. Allow your inner sight to see past the chatter of fear and doubt to a deeper truth.

....

....

....

....

....

....

....

"BOTH MODERN
PHYSICISTS AND
ANCIENT MYSTICS
CAN AGREE THAT
EVERYTHING IS IN A
STATE OF VIBRATION.
YOUR BODY IS LIKE
AN ORCHESTRA THAT
CAN BE TUNED WITH
SOUND."

–Jonathan Goldman

HEARING AND HEALING

Sounds of all kinds—music, tones, soft speech, frequencies that resonate with our bodies—can have a healing effect while reducing anxiety and depression. This morning, put on some of your favorite, relaxing sounds, no matter what they are, and sit in quiet meditation while listening to them. If you want to try something that's perhaps new to you, look online for bilateral music. Listen to it in headphones and notice as it shifts rhythmically back and forth from the left to right ear, which some people find energizing yet soothing.

As you listen, write or draw free-form in the space below.

GOOD MORNING, MINDFULNESS

One of the most amazing things about meditating in the morning is that it helps infuse your day with a mindful awareness. When you meditate, you bring focus to the present, to the beauty of the breath, to how good it feels to show up for yourself, to the joy of just being. As you develop your meditation practice, that focus on the now becomes a sort of undercurrent to your way of being. You become generally more aware and present in the moment.

Focus that mindful awareness on this very moment and write out the details of what you see around you using all of your senses. Maybe it's something small, like your sleeping pet or the mug you are sipping from, or something more ambitious, like the scene out the window.

....

....

....

....

....

....

....

A GOOD MORNING ON TAP

Tapping, also known as EFT (emotional freedom technique), is a simple practice that clears blockages to rebalance the energy in your body and help you overcome limiting beliefs. It's like a very gentle form of self-acupressure. To start, identify something you'd like to change, your "most pressing issue." Let's say you want to decrease your anxiety.

Write a few sentences that sum up the issue you'd like to work on, then express that you love and accept yourself despite the issue. This is your "setup statement." For example: "Even though I feel anxious and overwhelmed, I deeply love and accept myself." Come up with a shortened form of your setup statement: your "reminder phrase" and write it down. With our example, you might say "This anxiety..." or "I'm anxious and overwhelmed..."

....

....

....

Next, take one or two fingers and tap on the side of your hand while saying your reminder statement three times. Then assess how you feel.

....

....

....

....

The following illustration shows the eight points you'll be tapping on in sequence: 1. eyebrow, 2. side of eye, 3. under eye, 4. under nose, 5. chin, 6. collarbone, 7. under arm, and 8. top of head. Tap on each point several times, saying your reminder phrase out loud, before moving on to the next point. Once you've completed this cycle, assess how you feel. How does it compare to what you wrote earlier?

....

....

....

....

Continue tapping on the eight points in the sequence, if needed, until you feel the blocks around the issue beginning to clear.

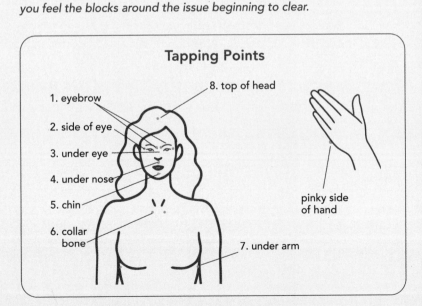

Tapping Points

1. eyebrow
2. side of eye
3. under eye
4. under nose
5. chin
6. collar bone

8. top of head

7. under arm

pinky side of hand

A MORNING GLIMMER OF TRANSCENDENTAL MEDITATION

*C*reated by Maharishi Mahesh Yogi in the 1950s (and practiced since by many celebrities, including the Beatles, Oprah Winfrey, and Jerry Seinfeld), Transcendental Meditation (TM) is based on the ancient Vedic belief that the universe is one Being, one ultimate reality. The meditation itself consists of sitting for 15 to 20 minutes per day and silently repeating a mantra specific to you, provided by an instructor, that allows your mind to effortlessly go into subtler and subtler layers of reality.

This morning you can get a taste for TM by picking a mantra you wrote earlier in this journal that feels good to you. Sit for a spell, silently repeating it in your mind. Allow yourself to become absorbed by the mantra for however long feels right—you can definitely build up to the lengthier 15-to-20-minute sessions.

How did this meditation feel? What do you think about trying it again in the future?

....

....

....

....

....

....

GOOD MORNING HERBS

There is a whole world of herbs out there (teas included) that can give you a boost of energy, help you focus, and make you more alert. The leaves in your average tea bag are ground up so fine they're practically powder, so it's worth getting loose tea for this meditation (or drying herbs yourself if you're a gardener). Buying loose tea allows you to experiment and come up with a custom blend tailored to your own tastes and needs. Here are some herbs that are particularly nice for starting the day:

Green tea and matcha are stimulating, caffeinated choices that are sure to start your day with just the right buzz, sans the jitters and late-morning crash of coffee.

Black tea is about half as caffeinated as coffee and comes in only about a million varieties.

Yerba maté comes from a species of South American holly and has more caffeine than most other herbs.

Peppermint is a caffeine-free way to fight fatigue, with an invigorating aroma that boosts mood and energy levels alike.

Schisandra is technically a berry and not an herb, but it's list-worthy for its energizing effects.

While we are only talking about the energizing aspects of these herbs, they also have myriad health benefits.

TEA UP A GOOD DAY

The simple act of brewing a cup of tea and sipping it in the morning can be a wonderfully mindful and meditative experience. All you need to do is tune in to what you're doing: Listen to the sounds of the water filling the kettle and coming to a bubbly boil. Feel the steam waft as you pour it into your mug. Smell the invigorating aroma of the tea. Then sit, enjoying the time it takes to cool off enough to drink, then savor each sip as a moment full of sensation and nourishment.

As you sip your tea, write in a stream of consciousness way here, freeing yourself from expectation and just writing for the relief and joy of it.

"[PAY] CLOSE ATTENTION TO YOUR DAY-TO-DAY LIFE, RECOGNIZING THE MOMENTS WHEN YOU FEEL FULLY ENGAGED AND PEACEFULLY INVOLVED. WHAT ARE YOU DOING? . . . NOTE WHEN YOU LAUGH, AND FEEL LIGHTHEARTED AND WEIGHTLESS IN YOUR SKIN."

–Sonia Choquette

FEED YOUR SPIRIT

*I*f you've been waking up feeling tired and disconnected (or even if you've been waking up feeling fantastic), take some time to feed your spirit. Start by noting the things that fill your cup—these are the things that make you laugh, make you feel like you're in the flow of the universe, and bring you joy. If they fill your cup, that's food for the spirit. Today, take as many opportunities as you can to feed your spirit.

List those things that fill your cup below and draw them in the cup on the next page.

....

....

....

....

....

....

....

....

continued . . .

What fills your cup? Draw it here.

ZEN OUT

A COUNTDOWN TO CALM

$\mathcal{B}$egin the day with a calm mind with this super-easy counting meditation. It's particularly good for those days when you have lots to do, and it's all racing through your mind as soon as you wake up, because it'll give you the calm confidence and focus you need to scratch all those items off the to-do list.

You can do this while sitting in your favorite position or even when you're still in bed. Close your eyes and take a steady breath in through your nose, down into your belly, and at the moment you shift to a slow exhale through your mouth, begin counting with "one." Repeat this up through 10 and then back down again as many times as you like. Or, you could list the colors of the rainbow, from energetic red to calming blue and purple; recite the alphabet; write a list of things you're grateful for and then say them aloud—whatever feels familiar and calming.

Now, write out your plan for the day, making sure to include some self-care!

....

....

....

....

....

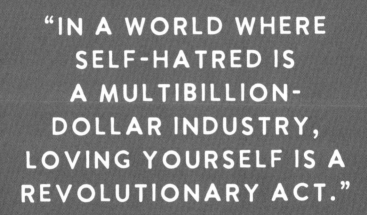

"IN A WORLD WHERE
SELF-HATRED IS
A MULTIBILLION-
DOLLAR INDUSTRY,
LOVING YOURSELF IS A
REVOLUTIONARY ACT."

–Gala Darling

START WITH RADICAL SELF-LOVE

With all the messaging in the world to sell you products that make you "better," it's no wonder many of us are far more used to self-doubt and self-criticism than self-love. These negative thoughts can become habit, but fortunately you can also make a habit of self-love with a simple meditation to start your morning off right!

Stand in front of a full-length mirror (either clothed or nude, your choice), and gaze into your eyes while taking a few steady breaths. Connect to yourself. Give yourself a warm smile and "good morning." Start to list all the things that are absolutely exquisite and wonderful about you, including the parts of your body that serve you so well and allow you to do all the things you need and love to do. You can do this silently or out loud.

Write them here and on the next page. Be sure to point out your favorite parts and give some extra kindness to any bits you may have been critical of in the past.

....

....

....

....

....

....

continued . . .

Keeping all of those positive, kind words in mind, sketch your gorgeous self here!

A CLEAN START

For a refreshingly meditative way to start the day, bring a little mindfulness into your morning routine, becoming aware of and immersed in something you sometimes rush or take for granted.

Let's try this with your morning shower. First, turn on the water and instead of waiting for it to get hot, hop in as soon as you can stand it. Feel that cool or even cold water as it brings your skin and senses to life! As you go through your normal steps to wash your body, take in the cleansing scents of your soap and shampoo. Feel the slippery textures. Watch the iridescent bubbles form and pop on your skin. Do your best to stay in the moment during this full-body sensory experience. If thoughts of the day start to break through, try counting up to 10 and back down with your breath or repeating an affirmation for the day silently or aloud.

How do you feel after your meditative shower? What is different now from before? Did this shower feel like a break from your regular morning routine?

....

....

....

....

....

....

DAILY BREAD

The phrase "daily bread," which comes from the New Testament of the Bible, captures the idea of how simple our everyday needs truly can be. Bread is symbolic of our basic needs. And while we can't actually live on bread alone, we can recognize what's really important to us—what we need to feel nourished and strong.

This morning, meditate and journal on what constitutes your daily bread—physically, spiritually, and otherwise.

....

....

....

....

....

....

....

....

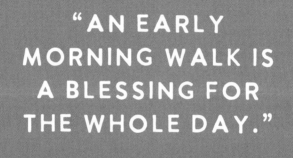

"AN EARLY
MORNING WALK IS
A BLESSING FOR
THE WHOLE DAY."

–Henry David Thoreau

WAKING, WALKING

There is something naturally meditative about a walk. This morning, go for a leisurely stroll. Try to focus your thoughts on the awakening world around you. Notice the sun playing on different surfaces, the sounds, the smells.

Write about what you felt, saw, heard, and smelled on your walk. On the next page, draw something striking you saw on your walk.

....

....

....

....

....

....

....

....

....

....

....

continued . . .

Draw something striking you saw on your walk.

ZEN OUT

MEDITATION BEADS

In many cultures and religions, people will chant or pray using beads to count off each round. In Catholicism, people will pray the rosary; in Islam the misbaha. Mahayana Buddhists use circles of prayer beads with a number of beads that is divisible by 108, while members of the Bahá'í Faith use a strand of 95 beads with 5 counters. Not only does this practice give you something tactile to focus on, but it also serves as a sort of timer. Instead of setting a clock or music to the length of time you want to meditate, you can make your way around the beads.

This morning, try meditating to a set of beads. These can be prayer beads, or a beaded necklace, or you can simply tie knots in a length of twine. For each bead, repeat a mantra or intention for the day.

How did you like this meditation? Did meditating using beads help you focus or add to your meditation?

....

....

....

....

....

....

Draw your prayer beads here.

"YOU'RE HERE TO SERVE.
YOU'RE HERE TO STOP
THINKING SO MUCH ABOUT
YOURSELF AND WHAT
OTHER PEOPLE THINK
ABOUT WHETHER YOU'RE
DOING THE RIGHT
THING. . . . GET OFF OF
ALL OF THAT. . . . ASK
YOURSELF THE QUESTION,
'HOW CAN I SERVE?'"

–Dr. Wayne Dyer

THE BEAUTY OF SERVICE

There's something about this modern moment in time that has made people turn inward. Maybe it's that we each have our own private screens, or maybe it's that social media has made us all into the stars of our own show, or maybe it's just how humans are and we just have more opportunities to do it these days. Regardless of the reasons, it is absolutely important to take care of yourself, but it's also important to turn that care outward so everyone can fill their cups to the top.

This morning, write about ways you could be of service to others, from small acts of kindness to as far as you care to take it.

....

....

....

....

....

....

....

....

BREAK IT GOOD

*B*ad habits are a real b-word: burden. They drag you down in so many ways and yet they're super hard to shake. But today is a new day! The day you take your first step toward breaking a habit you want to kick.

First, write about the habit and how you feel about it. Explore not only why it's tough to break it, but what that resistance feels like.

....

....

....

....

....

....

....

....

....

....

Now imagine yourself free of that habit. Close your eyes and visualize yourself well past it. How do you feel? Make the picture as clear and emotional as you can. Now, work backward. How did you get to that point? Write down all the steps, no matter how small, and then take the first one.

THE CHAKRAS

The chakras are energy centers in your body. When all is well, they spin freely clockwise and allow energy to flow completely through you. While there are thought to be as many as 78,000 chakras in the body, there are seven major ones:

 The crown chakra is your higher consciousness and is associated with your spirituality and the universe.

 The third-eye chakra is linked to intuition, imagination, and psychic abilities.

 The throat chakra relates to communication, creativity, and your truth.

 The heart chakra is filled with compassion and love.

 The solar plexus chakra is concerned with willpower and intellect.

 The sacral chakra is connected to emotions, sexuality, and creation.

 The root chakra (aka the base chakra) connects to the earth and embodies the survival instinct.

If one or more of these chakras are blocked, spinning counterclockwise, or overactive, it can throw off your whole system, making you feel sluggish, overwhelmed, or a whole host of other negative things. Meditation can help reopen chakras and get them spinning in the right direction.

A CHAKRA MEDITATION
FOR THE MORNING

When your chakras are completely opened and spinning optimally, you feel at one with the world. Use this meditation on those mornings when you're feeling a little off to bring you back to that sense of connectivity and oneness.

Start by positioning your body in your favorite meditation pose. Close your eyes and bring your attention to your breath. Imagine a red sun dawning and filling your legs and root chakra with red light. Picture that ball of light rising up and becoming orange as it lights up your sacral chakra. Now feel the ball of light as it moves up through your chakras, turning yellow at your solar plexus, green at your heart, blue at your throat, and indigo at your third eye. Then imagine white light beaming from the top of your head, opening up an energetic connection between you and the universe.

How did this meditation feel? Did you feel like you could sense your chakras? Did you notice any difficult areas or blockages?

"I THANK THE
EARTH MOTHER FOR
PROVIDING THIS
FOOD FOR ME, AND
I THANK THE FOOD
FOR GIVING ITS LIFE
TO NOURISH ME."

–Louise Hay

MIND YOUR BREAKFAST

Breakfast has long been known as the most important meal of the day because it gives you the energy you need to get moving. You can ramp up that energetic intake if you bring a little mindfulness to the meal. When you eat this morning, try to focus on the whole experience. The careful preparation, the experience of eating something so nourishing, the exchange of energy from the food to your body.

How was the experience? What are your own feelings of gratitude toward your food like? If you have a prayer or other form of recognition you use to honor your food, write it below.

continued . . .

What is your favorite breakfast? Draw it below. Surround it with the words and experiences you associate with it.

ZEN OUT

FIVE-MINUTE NO RULES

Sometimes you wake up and you just don't wanna. You didn't sleep well, you have too much going on, you're running late— whatever the reason may be, there will likely be days when you don't feel like meditating, especially when you're first building your practice. On these days, turn to the five-minute no rules meditation. Simply sit for five minutes with no agenda—that's it. Don't try to control your breath or your thoughts or your thoughts about your thoughts. Just let it all go for five minutes with no direction and no judgments, focusing on something like the breath only if you want to. Then get up and go about your day. Or continue to sit.

What gets in your way when it comes to meditating? How can you maneuver around those blocks?

....

....

....

....

....

....

FIND YOUR NATURAL RHYTHM

$\mathcal{S}$tart your day by getting in touch with your body's natural rhythm. Settle into your favorite meditation position, close your eyes, and notice your breath. Being conscious of it will, of course, change it. The mind's eye has that effect, and that's not a bad thing. Allow your attention to rest on the breath, which will go back to normal soon. Be as still as you can in the rest of your body.

Focus on the subtlest sensations of the breath. Feel the air as it travels from your nose into your lungs. Feel your lungs moving in your chest. Notice the rhythm there. Once you do, see if you can find your heartbeat in that rhythm. Feel for it behind your lungs. Perhaps imagine the sensation to see if you can draw it forward. You may want to keep a pencil in your hand and record the rhythms in the space below as they occur, acting as your own heart monitor. Or you can remember those rhythms and draw them when you're done. Stay here for as long as you like.

How did you feel exploring your rhythm? How deep did you go?

"THE CHIEF TASK IN LIFE IS SIMPLY THIS: TO IDENTIFY AND SEPARATE MATTERS SO THAT I CAN SAY CLEARLY TO MYSELF WHICH ARE EXTERNALS NOT UNDER MY CONTROL, AND WHICH HAVE TO DO WITH THE CHOICES I ACTUALLY CONTROL."

–Epictetus

GET STOIC

The Stoics were ancient Greek philosophers who had a . . . unique take on things. One of the beliefs they held was that bad things are going to come your way and usually there's nothing you can do about it. As part of this belief, they accepted that much of life is suffering (just like the Buddha did, unbeknownst to them). By taking this approach to life, they wouldn't be surprised or upset when confronted by situations that were out of their control. In other words, it doesn't serve you to get mad at the storm.

What upsets you but is totally out of your control? How does it feel to recognize your lack of control? Does it make you feel a hint of freedom, or do you want to shake your fist at the clouds?

....

....

....

....

....

....

....

ENERGIZING ESSENTIAL OILS

Adding a scent-scape to any meditation practice is beneficial, but it's really got some perks if you use it in the morning. There are many lovely oils that not only smell great, but also can fight fatigue and help you focus. Here are a few essential oils that will lift your spirit and get you geared up for your day.

 Mints: Peppermint and spearmint are known for their invigorating effects.

 Herbs: Rosemary can improve not just focus, but memory as well, while thyme can boost your energy.

 Spices: Black pepper and cinnamon are both sure to make your eyes open a little wider.

 Citrus: Pretty much any citrus scent—grapefruit, orange, lemon, you name it—will lift your mood and add some pep to your step.

Try mixing together a few drops of your favorite essential oils to make a personalized blend for your morning meditation.

MORNING MASSAGE ESSENTIALS

Massages aren't just for once-a-year spa days—you can get the same relaxing results on your own. Mix a couple drops of your favorite high-quality invigorating essential oil with a skin-friendly carrier oil like coconut or argan. Sit in your favorite meditation position and gently massage a bit of the oil blend into your hands as you inhale the uplifting aroma. If you like, you can also massage your feet, your temples, and/or your arms. Go slowly and feel the energy from the oil and the loving care you're giving yourself be absorbed through your skin and begin to circulate in your body.

What oil blend did you use? How do you feel after the massage and meditation versus before you started? Do you notice an increase in energy or feelings of self-love?

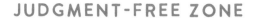

JUDGMENT-FREE ZONE

The mind loves to judge. That's what it's there for in a lot of ways, to figure out what's good and bad for you, always solving problems to keep you safe and help you thrive. Therefore, the problems you face are, in a sense, manufactured in the mind, and the true reality of the world around you is that it is a neutral place.

This morning, try meditating on that neutrality. Get into your favorite meditation position, close your eyes, and focus on the breath. If your mind wanders and you begin to judge yourself for not being able to focus perfectly or slow down your racing thoughts, just let that pass you by. Get into a judgment-free zone where you embrace the world as it is and yourself as you are.

How did you feel during this meditation? Were you able to let go of judgments, even if it was just for a little while?

DAY OF REST

No one can carry their load indefinitely. You sometimes need to drop everything and give yourself a rest so you can carry on without breaking down. Today, you're going to give yourself a rest from whatever burden you've been carrying. First, visualize your worries as harmless little knickknacks and draw them on these pages. If you like, you can give them labels or write down words you associate with them. You might picture a worry about a loved one as a framed photo of them or money worries as a piggy bank.

Then get into your favorite meditation position and close your eyes. Steady your breathing. Picture a big open box. Now start putting your knickknacks in the box. They're so light and easy to manage, and you don't need them right now. Once they're all safely inside, place a lid on the box. Then pick up the box—it's so light and easy to carry—and put it on a shelf in the closet. Now close the closet door and open your eyes.

Your cares are going to stay in the closet today. If one breaks out, just close your eyes and envision putting it back in the box in the closet. Tomorrow you can unpack the box—and perhaps you'll leave a few things in there for a while longer.

Draw your box on the next page and either write or draw some of your worries inside it. Then close this journal and forget about them for the rest of the day.

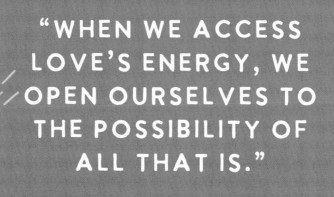

"WHEN WE ACCESS
LOVE'S ENERGY, WE
OPEN OURSELVES TO
THE POSSIBILITY OF
ALL THAT IS."

–James Van Praagh

LOVE IT!

*A*ccess love's energy this morning and all the possibilities it brings! Start by writing a list of people you treasure and what you love about them.

Then, get into your favorite meditation position, close your eyes, and settle down. Think about those people and allow yourself to really feel the love you have for them. Let that love fill your chest and lift the corners of your mouth into a smile. Picture each person as clearly as you can and send that feeling of love out to them. Once you've gone through the people on your list, send that feeling of love out to your street, your town, and your state, then let it radiate out to the country and the world. Finally, send that really big love to yourself.

Write that list of people here. How did it feel to make this list and consciously send out love to each person?

....

....

....

....

....

....

IT'S A BEAUTIFUL MORNING

Take a look around and notice all the beauty that's there with you in so many forms, both inside and outside of you, and the unity in between and in the vibration. Activate all your senses, noticing the visual beauty but also how the air feels and smells, what you hear, and what you taste. Meditate on this, then write about it here.

....

....

....

....

....

....

....

....

....

....

....

....

....

JOY MULTIPLICATION

This morning list all the really big things that bring you joy, like love or nature or music, but leave a few line spaces between each one. Once you have your big list, then jot down the little things within the big things that bring you joy. Go on to add the little joys from those things. See how many factors of joy you can deduce from each big source of joy.

Hay House Titles of Related Interest

YOU CAN HEAL YOUR LIFE, the movie,
starring Louise Hay & Friends
(available as an online streaming video)
www.hayhouse.com/louise-movie

THE SHIFT, the movie,
starring Dr. Wayne W. Dyer
(available as an online streaming video)
www.hayhouse.com/the-shift-movie

* * *

The High 5 Daily Journal,
by Mel Robbins

Living Your Purpose Journal,
by Dr. Wayne W. Dyer

The Sacred Cycles Journal,
by Jill Pyle, Em Dewey, and Cidney Bachert

All of the above are available at your local bookstore,
or may be ordered by contacting Hay House (see next page).

* * *

SOURCES

Page 10: *The Golden Louise Hay Collection*
Page 20: *A Fierce Heart*
Page 34: "Morning Meditation for Healing" from Hay House Audio App
Page 40: *Trust Life*
Page 46: Quoting her teacher on "If This Is You, It Is Time to Let It Go" from Hay House Audio App
Page 54: *The Power of Surrender*
Page 62: *The 7 Secrets of Sound Healing*
Page 74: *Ask Your Guides*
Page 80: "A Simple Plan to Achieve Radical Self-Love"
Page 94: "Get Through Tough Times by Helping Others" from Hay House Radio
Page 102: *You Can Heal Your Life*
Page 120: *The Power of Love*